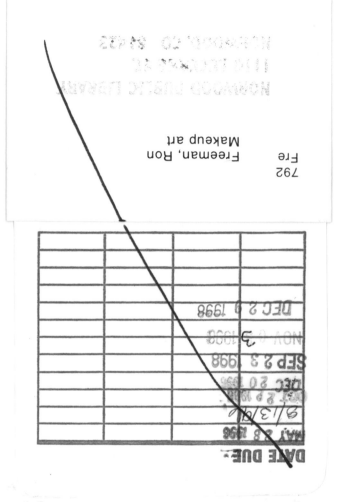

MAKEUP ART

Ron Freeman

Consultant: Henry Pluckrose

Photography: Chris Fairclough

FRANKLIN WATTS
New York/London/Sydney/Toronto

Franklin Watts Inc
387 Park Avenue South
New York NY 10016

Library of Congress Cataloging-in-Publication Data

Freeman, Ron.
    Makeup Art / Ron Freeman.
       p.   cm. — (Fresh start)
    Includes index.
    Summary: Photographs and step-by-step pictures reveal how
theatrical makeup can create faces of clowns, robots, animals,
dolls, and the elderly. Includes suggestions for further activities
and information on both suppliers and the techniques of
professionals in the field.
    ISBN 0-531-14133-0
    1. Make-up, Theatrical—Juvenile literature.   [1. Makeup.
Theatrical.]   I. Title.
PN2068.F68   1991
792'.027—dc20   90-38305
                                                 CIP   AC

Design: K & Co

Editor: Jenny Wood

Typeset by Lineage

Printed in Belgium
All rights reserved
Acknowledgement
The author and publisher would
like to thank the following young
people who have been used in the
illustrations: Amy Lynn; Stefan
Radwanski; Danny Sweetman;
Emma Tingle.

Contents

This book describes activities which use the following:

Bald caps
Brushes (shading and powder, see page 5)
Chair
Cotton balls
Crêpe hair
Diamanté tears
Eyebrow pencils
Eyelash glue
"Kryolan" hairspray (colored)
Mirror (large)
Mixing palette
Newspaper
Paper tissues
Paper towels
Pencils (lead and colored for initial designs)

Rouge powder
Scissors
Sheets (old, for covering model and table)
Sketch pad (for initial designs)
Soap (for washing hands/face)
Sponges
Spirit gum
Spirit gum remover
Table
Theatrical makeup colors: – Kryolan (Aqua Color)
Toothbrush
Towels
Wastebasket
Water
Water jar

Keep your makeup in a strong box.

1 Makeup, a basic kit.

Getting started

This book has been written to encourage you to experiment with colors which can safely be used, at home or at school, to "make up" the face. Whether you want to disguise yourself at a fancy dress party or you are thinking of taking part in a drama production at school or at your youth club, the pages that follow will teach you how to use water-based colors to change your appearance – and that of your friends!

A number of different makeups are featured. Each illustrates the processes you will need to master. Although the processes are important, you do not need to follow the designs exactly. Being creative is not just following instructions! The creative person takes an idea, experiments, and in so doing achieves something which is his or her own.

Equipment

All the colors described in this book are water-based. They can be applied on a damp sponge, or with a brush. "Kryolan" colors can be bought from any store that sells theatrical makeup, and are sold singly or in boxed sets. For beginners, I suggest that a basic set, containing a range of colors, is the best buy. You will also need some cakes of "Aqua Color." These are essential for preparing a base on which to work and are available in a range of colors.

Several types of brushes are used in makeup. You will need some shading brushes (Sizes 6, 8 and 10) and some powder brushes. A powder brush has a large, soft head. In your makeup kit you will require a 1.2cm (½ inch) round-headed powder brush and a 1.2cm (½ inch) chisel-headed powder brush.

In many designs, it will be necessary to conceal the model's hair. This is easily achieved by using a bald cap (also available from stores that sell theatrical makeup). The cap is held in position with spirit gum.

Some hints

Applying makeup can be back-breaking work. Make sure that your model (the person who is to be made up) sits on a chair with a high seat. Raise your model if necessary by putting a thick, firm cushion (or even a box) on the seat of the makeup chair.

Remember, your model will need to be comfortable. Makeup cannot be applied quickly and the model may have to sit still for quite a long time.

1 Place a table in front of the makeup chair. Set out on the table all the materials you will need. Your makeup mirror should also stand on the table.

2 The mirror is an essential piece of equipment. When you make up a model you will need to glance continuously into the mirror to see how your design is developing, to make sure that the features on each side of the face balance and that the colors are evenly applied.

3 The table arranged for working.

Like most craft activities, applying face makeup can be a little messy. Be prepared for mess before you make it. Use an old sheet or cloth to cover the table. Place a wastebasket near the makeup chair, for waste material. The model will need covering, too – a sheet or towel over his or her shoulders will be sufficient. When not using a bald cap, keep the model's hair off his or her face with a stocking or hairband.

The water-based makeup used in the examples which follow is easy to remove, but you will have to make sure that you have access to soap, towels and a ready supply of hot water. If moustaches and beards are part of the makeup, you will also require spirit gum remover. Never apply makeup if there is no way of removing it safely and easily. Cleansing is essential.

Finally, before you begin to work on a model, be sure that you know the design you are to follow. Always begin with a sketch. Some of the drawings prepared for the designs in this book are included in the text.

7

A doll

You will need a sponge, "Aqua Color" shade 4W, blue powder makeup, shading brushes, rouge powder, a powder brush, black and red "Kryolan" colors, and an eyebrow pencil.

1 A sketch of the design.

2 Dampen the sponge and use it to apply "Aqua Color" (shade 4W) to the face and the neck to just below the costume line.

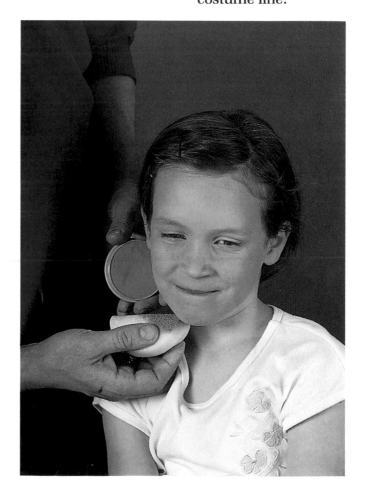

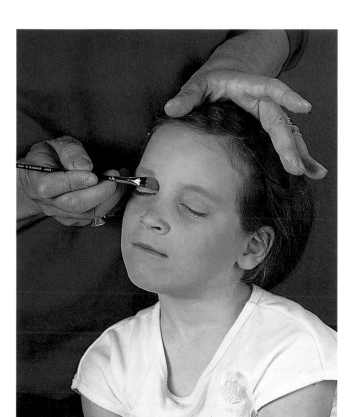

3 Now make up the eyelids using the blue powder makeup.

4 Apply rouge to the cheeks with the powder brush.

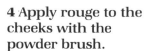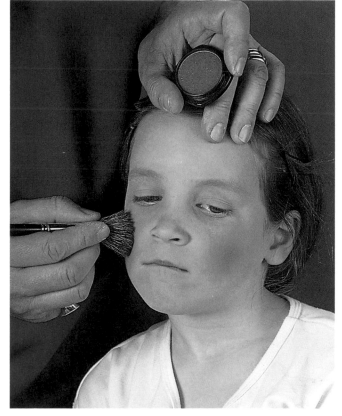

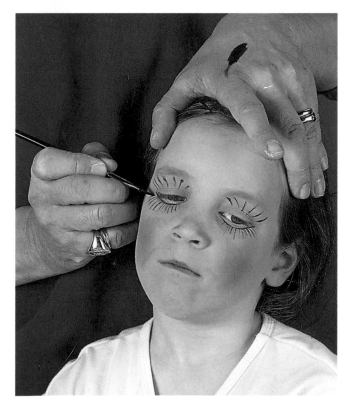

5 Eyes are very important features in all face makeup. Black "Kryolan" emphasizes the eye line...

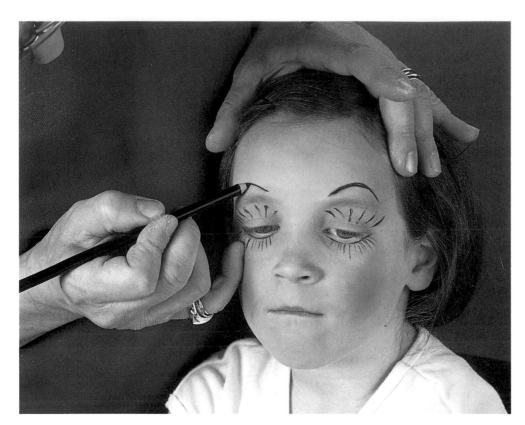

6 ... and the eyebrow pencil is used to strengthen the eyebrows.

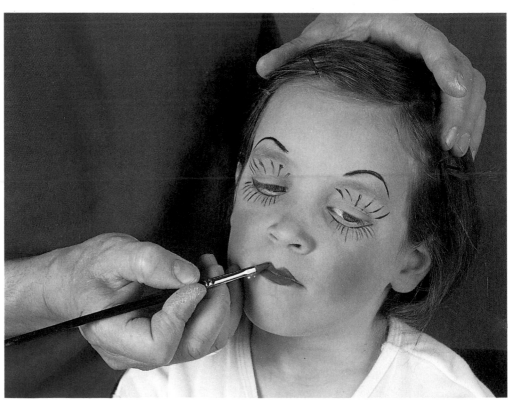

7 Finally, paint the lips with red "Kryolan."

8 *The Doll.* Compare the finished result with the original sketch...

9 ... and with this photograph of Amy, the model.

You will need a bald cap, scissors, spirit gum, sponges, white "Aqua Color," "Kryolan" colors in various shades according to your design, and shading brushes (Size 6).

1 A sketch of the design.

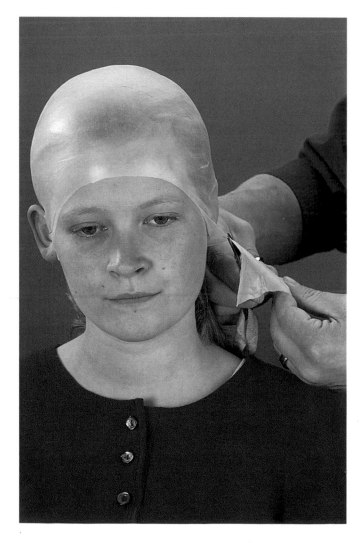

2 For this design, the model's hair must be taken away from the face using the bald cap. The cap is cut away around the eyes, and slots are made for the ears. Using a damp sponge or wet towel, apply spirit gum around the edges of the cap to hold it in position on the head. Don't use your fingers!

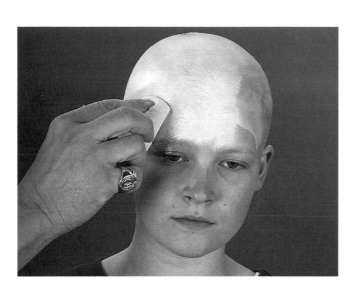

3 Using a damp sponge, apply white "Aqua Color" evenly around the join by dabbing...

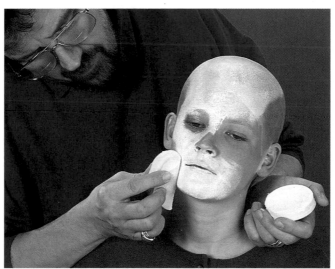

4 ... all over the face, ...

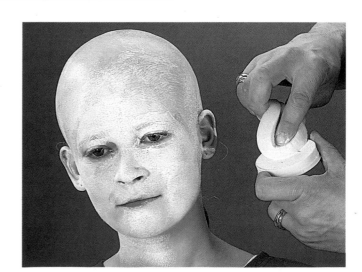

5 ... over the bald cap and around the neck. Try to avoid any uneven patches of color.

6 Now decorate the face with "Kryolan" colors applied by brush. Work from the eyes outward. Look in the mirror to make sure that the design is identical on both sides of the face.

7 The advantage of "Kryolan" colors is that you can work one color after the other without waiting for the first color to dry. If you make a mistake, just wipe off the paint and start again. Sometimes the "mistakes" can be made into part of your design!

8 Color the lips.

9 The completed design. Compare the finished result with the original sketch...

10 ... and with this photograph of Emma, the model.

You will need a bald cap, scissors, spirit gum, a damp sponge, black, red, and white "Kryolan" colors, and shading brushes.

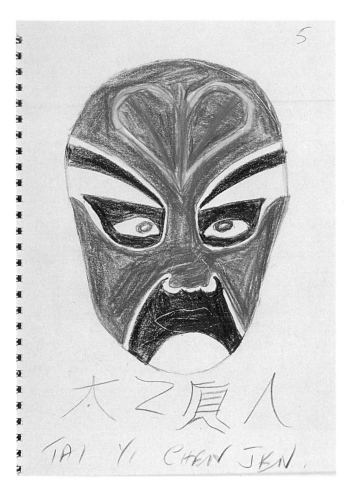

1 A sketch of the design.

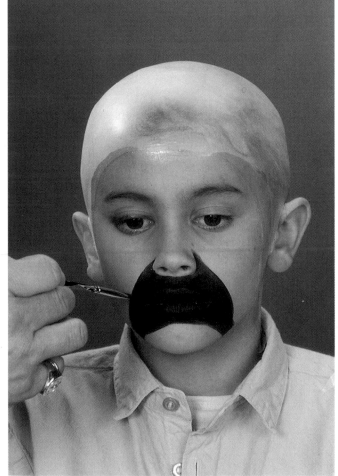

2 Cover the hair with the bald cap. Shape it around the ears and fix it in position with spirit gum. (See page **12.**)

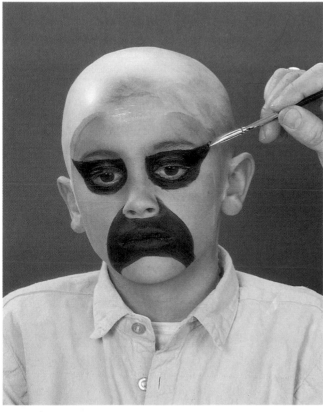

3 Color the mouth and eyes with black "Kryolan."

4 Whiten the chin, nostrils and the area around the eyes.

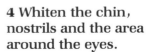

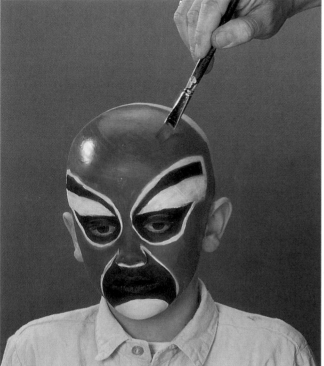

5 Cover the rest of the face with red "Kryolan," using a brush.

6 The completed design. Compare the finished result with the original sketch...

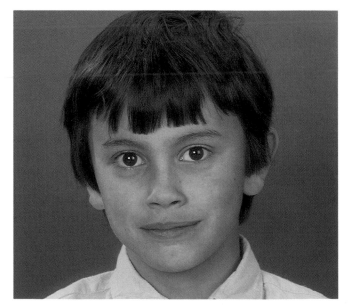

7 ... and with this photograph of Danny, the model.

This design does not require a sketch. You will need a bald cap, spirit gum, sponges, gold and black "Aqua Color", and a shading brush.

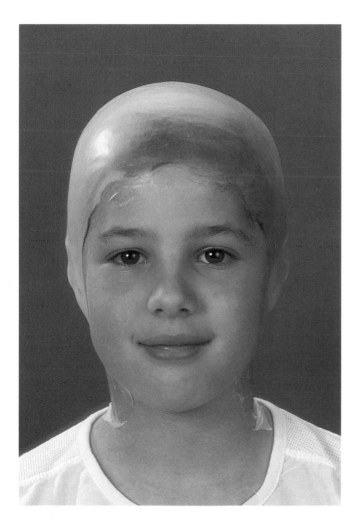

1 Begin by covering the hair and ears with the bald cap. Fix it in position with spirit gum (see page 12).

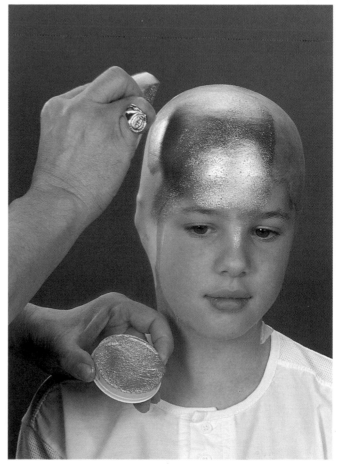

2 Now apply gold "Aqua Color" all over the head, face...

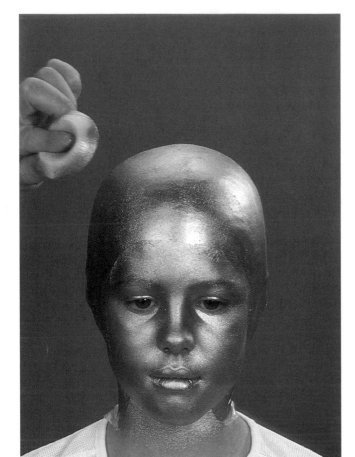

3 ... and neck, using a damp sponge.

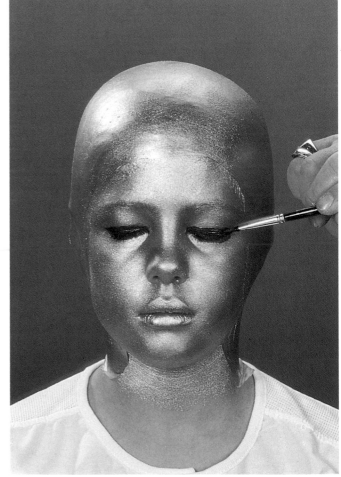

4 Final details around the nostrils and eyes are added in black "Kryolan," applied by brush. Experiment with your own robot makeup ideas.

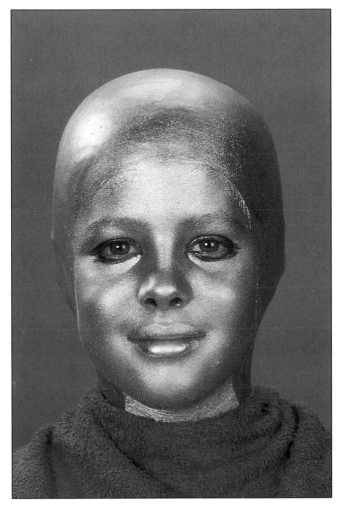

5 The completed design.

6 Compare the finishcd rcsult with this photograph of Stefan, the model.

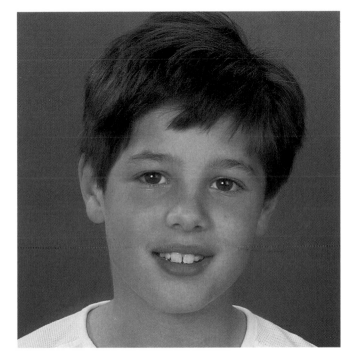

7 Many strange creatures can be found in the studios of a theatrical makeup artist!

This is a traditional design and a sketch should not be necessary. You will need a bald cap, scissors, spirit gum, sponges, white "Aqua Color," black, and red "Kryolan" colors, shading brushes, a diamanté tear, and eyelash glue.

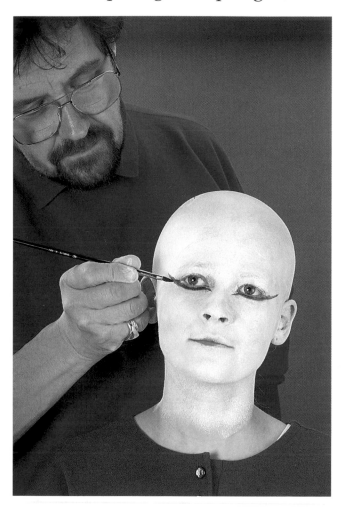

1 Cover the hair with the bald cap. Shape it around the ears and keep it in position with spirit gum. (See page 12.) Now cover the face and cap with a layer of white "Aqua Color" applied by dabbing with a damp sponge. Outline the eyes with black "Kryolan."

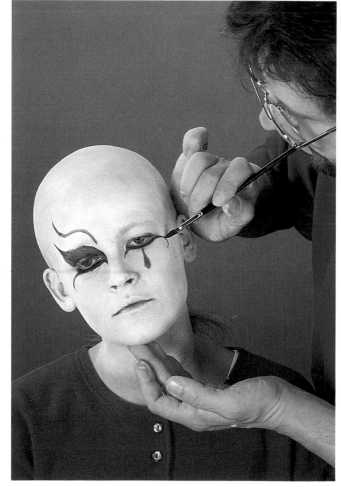

2 Add more black "Kryolan" around the eyes, and add a dark tear drop.

3 Use the black "Kryolan" to emphasize the line of the lips, too.

4 Color the lips with red "Kryolan."

5 Add the diamanté tear last of all. Coat the back of the tear lightly with eyelash glue and place it on the cheek.

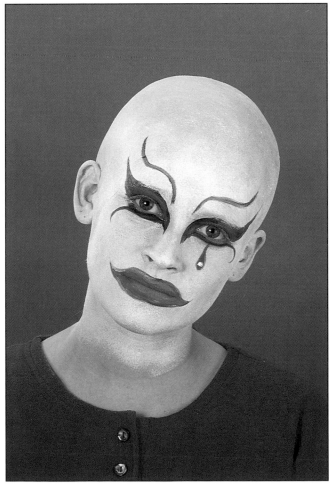

You will need a bald cap, spirit gum, sponges, gray, purple, lilac, and black "Kryolan" colors, a palette, water, a 1.2cm (½ inch) flat-headed shading brush, a lip brush, an eyebrow pencil, a length of crêpe hair, a sheet of newspaper, and "Kryolan" hairspray.

1 A sketch of the design.

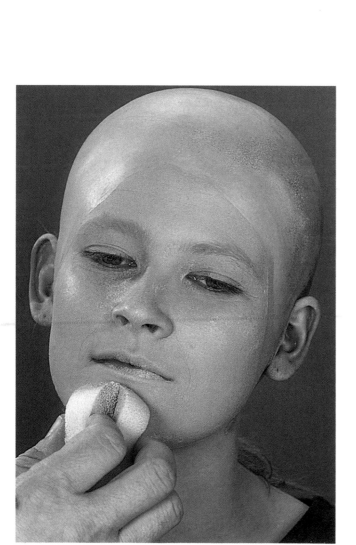

2 Cover the hair with the bald cap. Shape it around the ears and fix it in position with spirit gum. (See page 12.) Apply gray "Kryolan" over the cap and the face, using a damp sponge.

3 The eye color was made by mixing together purple and lilac "Kryolan." Put some of each color onto the palette, add a little water and mix the colors together. Add more purple or lilac as required, to obtain the exact shade. Use the shading brush to apply the eye color.

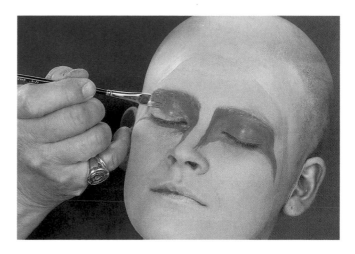

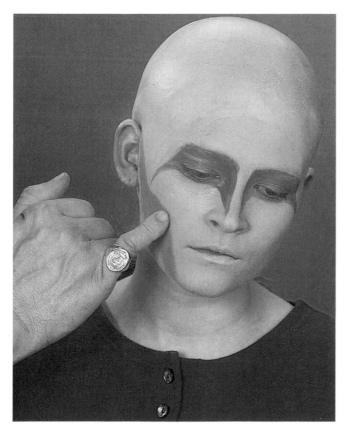

4 Decorate the cheeks with the same colors. Blend in the dry colors with your fingertips.

5 Paint the lips black and line the eyes with the eyebrow pencil. In a design like this, it is not necessary to make both sides of the face identical.

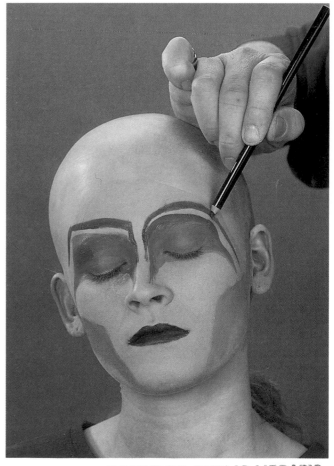

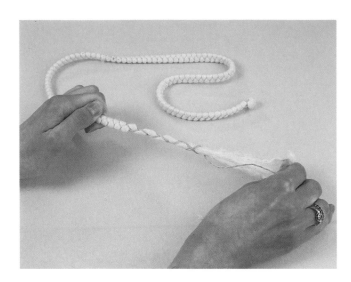

6 Now untie the length of crêpe hair.

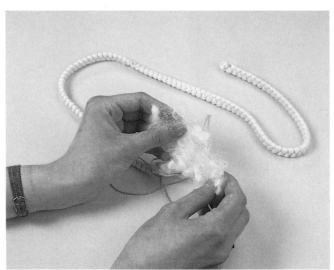

7 Make your length of hair fluffy by pulling and teasing it between your fingers.

8 Place the fluffed-out piece of hair on a sheet of newspaper. Color with "Kryolan" hairspray.

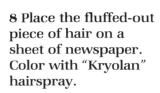

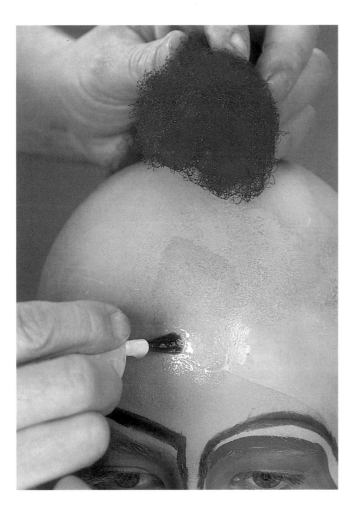

9 Put a line of spirit gum on the bald cap and position the hair length on it.

10 The completed design. Compare this with the original sketch. Which of the four models was used for the punk?

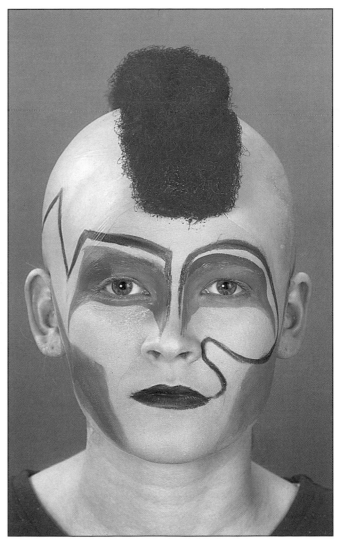

You will need "Aqua Color" shade 4W, a damp sponge, rouge powder, a 1.2cm (½ inch) powder brush, shading brushes, brown, light-red, ivory, carmine and highlight "Kryolan" colors, an eyebrow pencil, and a small toothbrush.

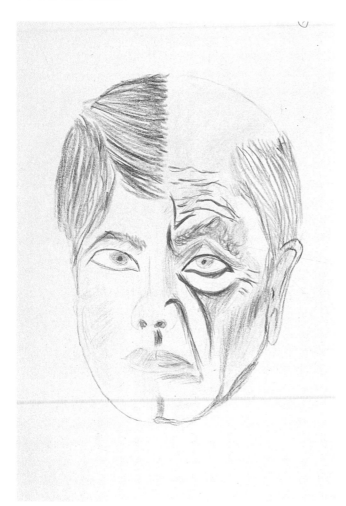

1 A sketch of the design, showing how one face can be made to look both young and old.

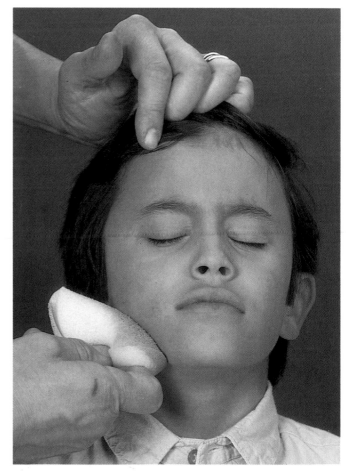

2 Give the whole face a natural base color ("Aqua Color," shade 4W).

3 Begin on the side of the face which is to show youth. Apply rouge powder with the powder brush to highlight the cheeks.

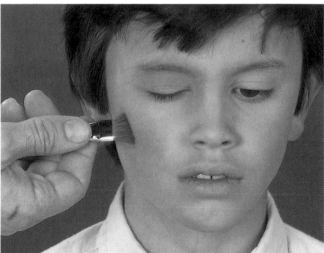

4 Emphasize the eyeline and eyebrow. Use brown "Kryolan" for the eyeline and the eyebrow pencil for the eyebrow.

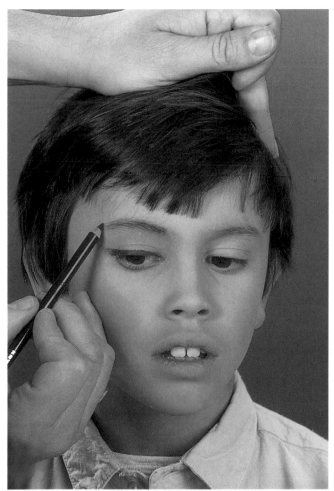

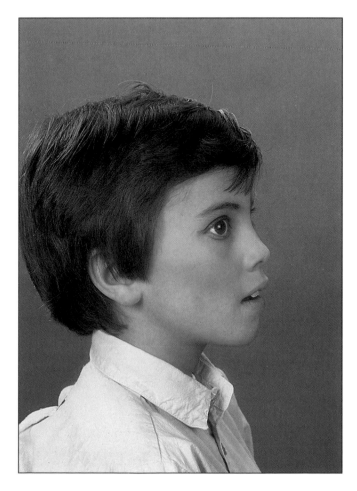

5 The young face.

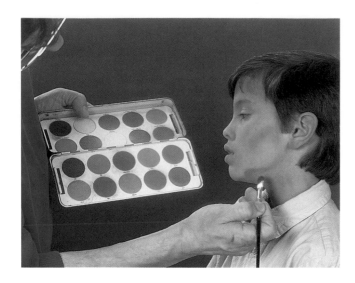

6 Now work on the side of the face which is to show age. Apply "Kryolan" brown shadow-color with a brush. Remember to darken the area beneath the cheekbone. Highlight the center line of the nose, the nostril and the eyelid with highlight color (applied in powder form).

7 The eye will need to look red and baggy. Lines of carmine, light red and brown will achieve this effect.

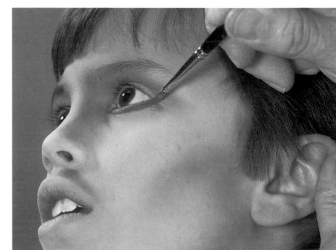

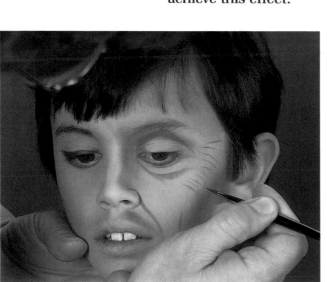

8 Add crease lines around the nose and mouth using brown "Kryolan" applied by brush.

9 Make the eyebrow bushy by brushing it with ivory "Kryolan" applied on the small toothbrush.

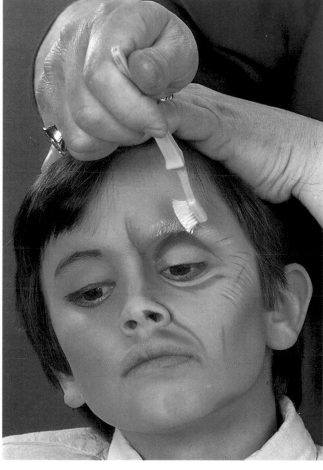

10 Ivory "Kryolan" can also be used to make dark hair look old and gray. Ivory is always used for this because white looks blue under stage lights and on people with very dark hair.

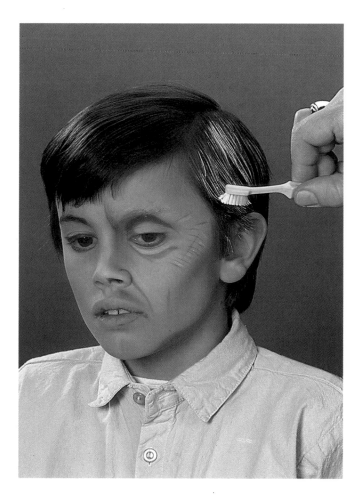

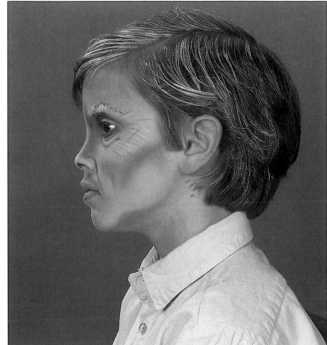

11 The old face.

12 The completed design. Compare this with the original sketch.

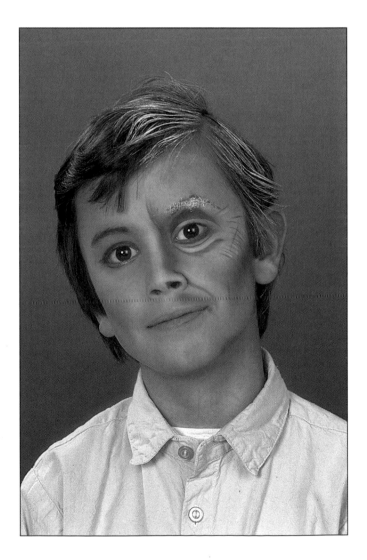

You will need a bald cap, spirit gum, sponges, white "Aqua Color," black and brick red "Kryolan" colors, a 1.2cm (½ inch) powder brush and a shading brush (Size 6).

1 A sketch of the design.

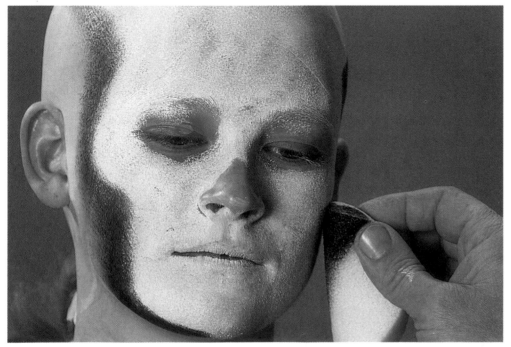

2 Cover the hair with the bald cap and fix it in position with spirit gum. (See page 12.) Apply white "Aqua Color" over the cap and face, leaving the nose and eye areas clear. Add a shading of black "Kryolan" to the white areas around the edge of the face to define the shape of the skull.

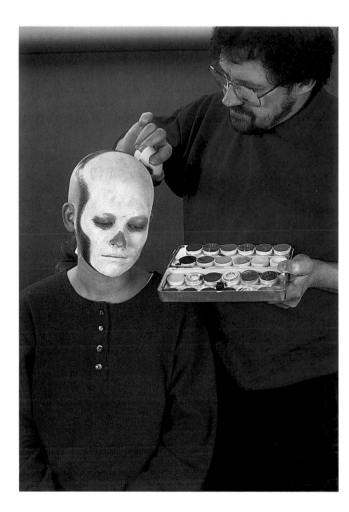

3 Mottle the white areas with brick red "Kryolan." Using a sponge, dab on the color so that the white surface is made to look old and decayed.

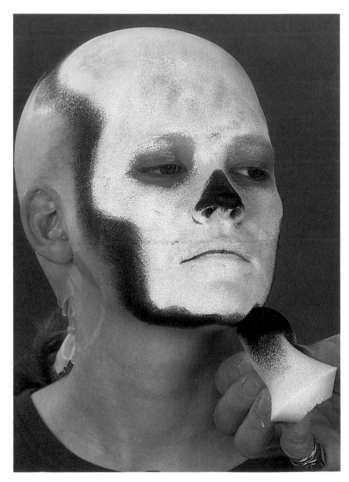

4 Black out the nose...

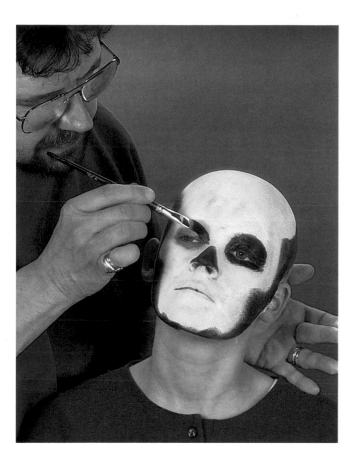

5 ... and, using the powder brush, darken the eye sockets.

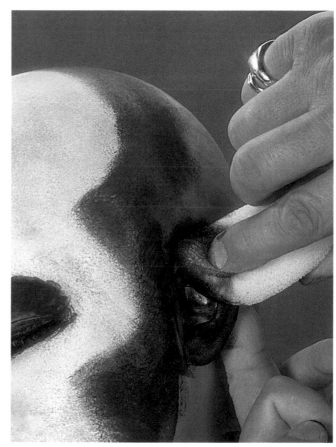

6 The ears will need to be blacked out too, or they can be left under the bald cap.

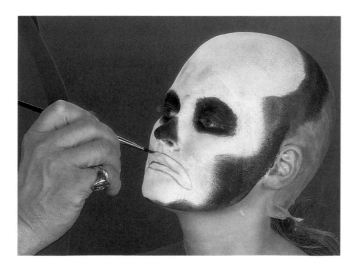

7 Now paint the mouth line, using the shading brush, ...

8 ... and add a broken line of teeth.

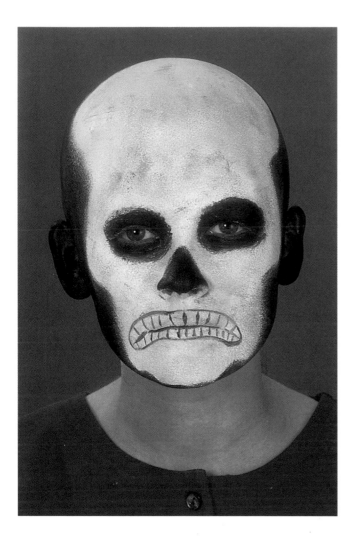

9 The completed design. Compare this with the original sketch.

You will need red, ginger, gold, pink, and white "Kryolan" colors, and a shading brush (Size 6).

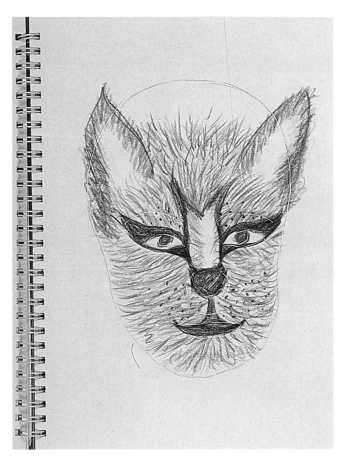

1 A sketch of the design.

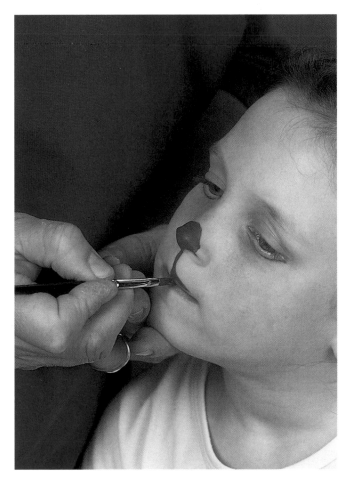

2 No base color is required for this design. Begin with the nose, applying red "Kryolan" with the shading brush. Notice that the nose line runs into the lips.

3 The eye shape must be that of an animal, not a human!

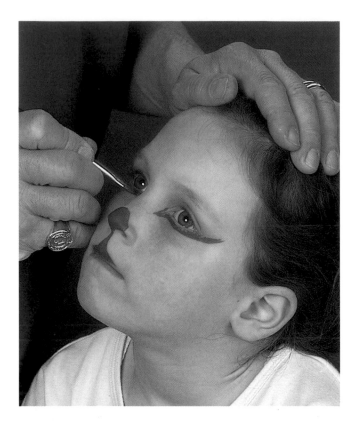

4 Lines above and below the eyes will help achieve this effect.

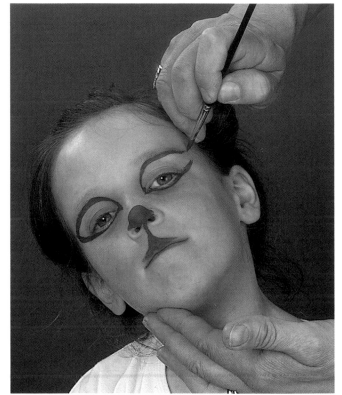

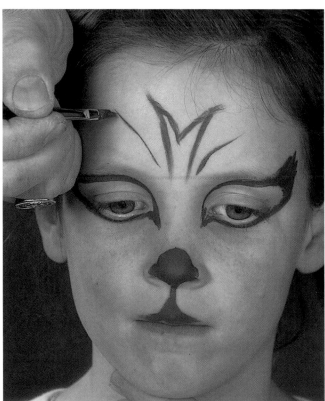

5 Begin to draw in the fur.

6 First texture the face with ginger lines then with lines of gold.

7 Finally add pink and white color to the mouth line and to the eyelids.

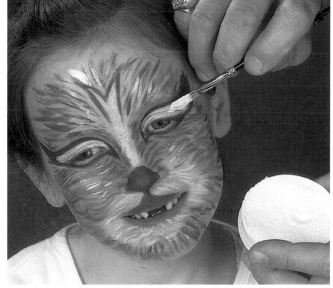

8 The completed design. Compare this with the original sketch and with the photograph of Amy on page 11.

You will need a bald cap, spirit gum, a damp sponge, black, brown, and white "Kryolan" colors, brushes, and an eye pencil.

1 A sketch of the design.

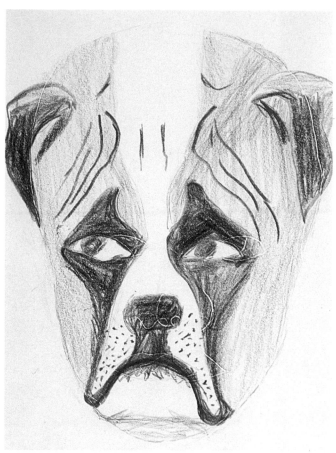

2 Cover the hair and ears with the bald cap and fix it in position with spirit gum. (See page 12.) Color the eyes with black "Kryolan," extending the design above and below the eye sockets.

3 Now add detail to the nose...

4 ... and lips.

5 Color the sides of the head with brown "Kryolan."

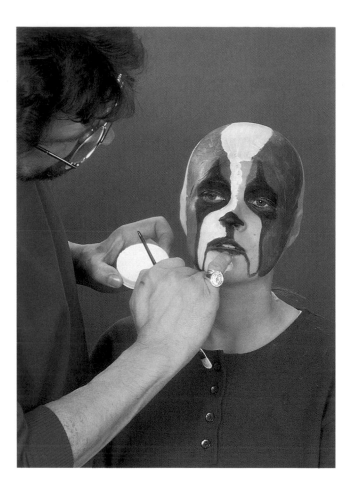

6 Use white "Kryolan" to fill the areas which remain uncovered. Use the tip of a brush to sharpen and define the white edge.

7 Use the eye pencil for whiskers...

8 ... and facial lines.

9 The completed design. Compare this with the original sketch and with the photograph of Emma on page 15.

On your own

Here are some other sketches
which you might like to use as
the basis for designs of your own.

1 Old Lady.

2 The Duchess.

3 *Spirit.*

4 *The Devil.*

5 A design in brick red.

Getting clean again

Water-based colors are as easy to remove as they are to apply.

Begin by softening any areas where spirit gum has been used with spirit gum remover. Apply the remover on a cotton ball. When the gum is soft, false hair (beards, moustaches) and the bald cap can be gently eased away from the skin. If the skin remains a little sticky when the hair or cap has been removed, clean off any gum which remains with the remover.

The paint is removed by washing with soap and hot water. It is best to wash the face several times – using fresh water – drying it between washes on paper towels. Use cotton balls to clean around the ears and around the eyes and nose.

Finally, when your model looks clean, wash once more to make sure every trace of paint has disappeared! It is an unwritten rule that actors never leave the theater with stage makeup on.

Suppliers

All the materials in this book can be obtained from:

Alcone Co. Inc.
Paramount Theater Supplies
5-49, 49th Avenue,
Long Island City, New York, NY 11101

Kryolan Corporation
132, Ninth Street
San Francisco
California 94103

Cosmoprof Investment PTE Ltd
1, Selegie Road
Paradiz Centre No 03-03
Singapore 0718

Fancy Dress Hire
Penelope Familton
1338 Onehunga Mall
P.O. Box 13-502
Onehunga, New Zealand

Malabar Ltd
14, McPaul Street
Toronto 28
Ontario, Canada

Back-Stage
Shop 3, Mid City Arcade
200, Bourke Street
Melbourne
Victoria 3000, Australia

PRINTED IN BELGIUM BY

INTERNATIONAL BOOK PRODUCTION